R. CRUMB

THE COMPLETE
RECORD COVER COLLECTION

W·W·NORTON

NEW YORK · LONDON

R. Crumb: The Complete Record Cover Collection not only brings together the record covers designed by Robert Crumb, but also includes works related to these covers.On top of that we added some lesser-known illustrations which are in some way related to the music. The majority of the covers were lent to us by Richard Kuiters and Cecile van Lijnden, Crumb-collectors for almost as long as there were Crumbs to collect.

Pierre-Henry Lenfant has shared with us the results of his research and also came up with a number of very rare works of which existence we had no idea.

Andreas Schmauder, Robert Armstrong, Dominic Cravic, Hansje Joustra and Joost Swarte provided us with a number of very special documents. When we thought we finally had completed the collection, Robert Crumb shattered this illusion by conjuring up some more editions.

When we started this collection we pretended full coverage, but the experience learned that this is a hard to reach goal. Now we are happy to live with the expectation that somewhere in a dusty drawer virtually unknown Robert Crumb covers and music related works are still waiting to be exposed.

the publisher

1   Why I'm Neurotic About My Record Collection, R. Crumb, Yazoo, 2006.

2   Musical Ecstasy at Age Four, drawing, 2004.

Monsieur Crumb, le soixante dix huitard

Tempo di java

Music and lyrics: Dominic Cravic

Quand vient l'di- manche ma- tin a la porte de Saint- Ouen le v'la par- ti en

Chi- ne qu'il gele ou bien qu'il fasse bon il ne porte qu'un ves-

ton en guise de ga- bar- di- ne d'un tas de noi- res ga-

le- ttes il de- terre un bi- dul' chouet- te

c'est bien le Roi du phono c'est Be- bert- Cha-

peau C'est la vraie val- se mu- se- tte

qui lui fait tour- ner la te- te l'plus fran- cais des

a- mer-los c'est Be- bert- Cha- peau

Rather than writing an ordinary preface, I preferred this 'java' presenting Robert Crumb in his favourite activity (second ? to drawing): scouring the flea markets for 78 records. "BEBERT CHAPEAU" is the nickname given to him by his neighbours in France, where he has been living for three years now, somewhere between Nîmes and Montpellier, with his two little girls Aline and Sophie.

June 1994.

3   Bedrock One,
event flyer/poster, 1967.

4   Illustration used for invitation
for the Grand Prix of the city
Angoulême, France, 2000.

6   Three buttons, Pinback Jack, 1972.

5   Larry Groce, Turn On Your TV,
Warner Bros Records. 7" record cover, 1977.
Lettering is added by the publisher.

7   Unknown Detroit Bluesmen
Volume 1, various artists, Barrelhouse.
12" record cover, 1970.

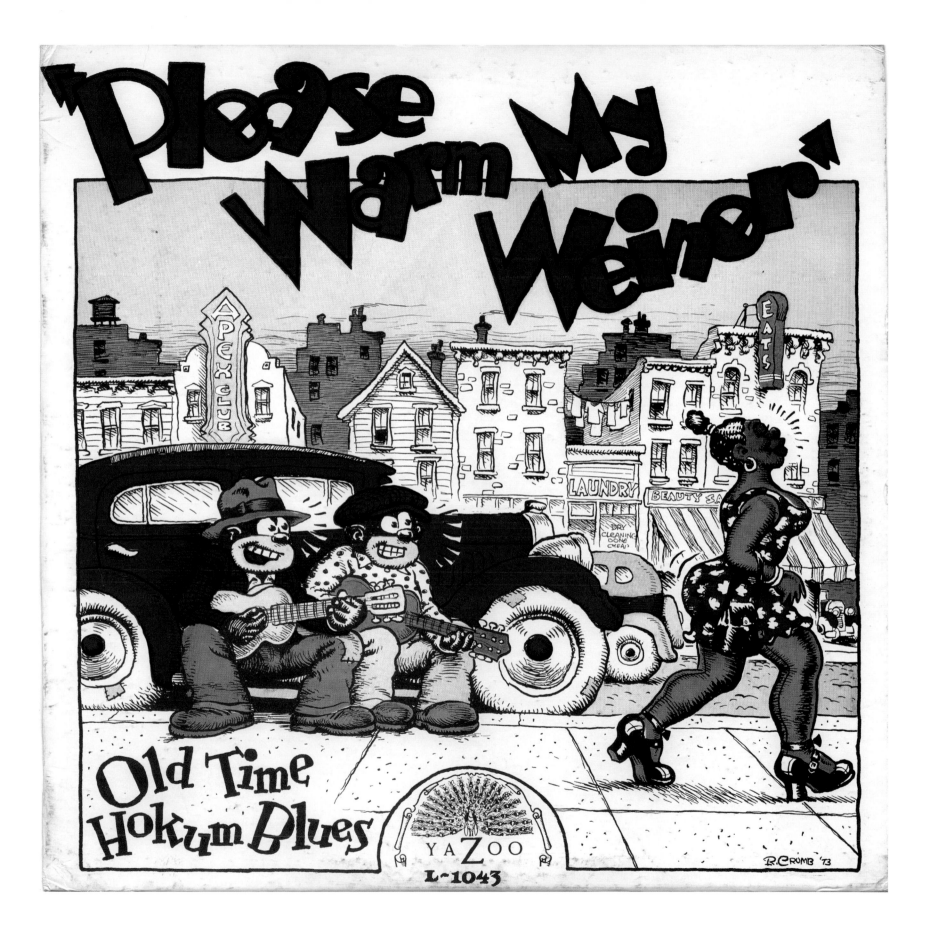

10 Ain't No Stopper On My
Faucet, Mama!, Unknown
Detroit Blues, various artists,
Barrelhouse.
12" record cover, 1970.

11 Oboy, drawing for a record
label, never published, 1973.

12 Oboy! It's Another Oboy
Record!, drawing for a record
cover commissioned by Apex
Novelty Co., never published, 1973.

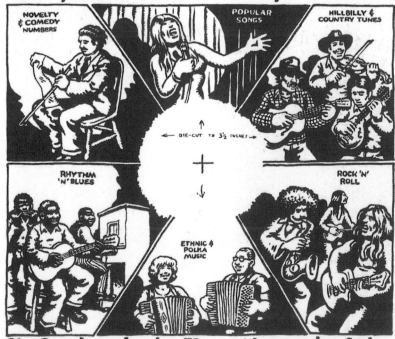

8 Drawing for a record cover
commisioned by Barrelhouse,
never published, 1970.

9 "Please Warm My Weiner", Old
Time Hokum Blues, various artists,
Yazoo. 12" record cover, 1973.

13 Ordinary, "A High Standard of Standardness", Krupp Comic Works. 10" record cover, 1972.

14 Ordinary, "River Blues", R. Crumb and His Keep-On-Truckin' Orchestra, Krupp Comic Works, record label, 1972.

15 Advertisement for The Ordinary Record!, Krupp Comic Works, Milwaukee, Wisconsin, 1972.

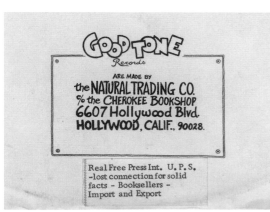

20   Harmonica Blues, Great Harmonica Performances of the 1920s and '30s, various artists, Yazoo. 12" record cover, 1976.

16   Good Tone Records, "Music Self-Played Is Happiness Self-Made!!", Good Tone Record Co., 10" record cover, 1972.

17   Good Tone, Beautiful Missouri Waltz, Armstrong's Pasadenians, Good Tone Record Co., record label 1972.

18   Two record labels as illustration to the short story: The Origins of Mr. Natural, Mr. Natural, Apex Novelties, 1970.

19   Lettering on backside of the above record cover.

21   Lettering for a 12" record cover:
I Got Dem Ol' Kozmic Blues Again
Mama!, Janis Joplin. Columbia. 1969.

22   Recycled Records, advertisement
for a record store, 1972.

• RARE & OUT OF PRINT ITEMS   • LPs 8-TRACK TAPES
• BUY · SELL AND TRADE   • CASSETTES · Some 78's · 45's

5051 Auburn Blvd., Sacramento, Ca. 95841 - 331-5900

23   Portrait of Janis Joplin,
silkscreen in a limited edition, 2008.

24   Janis Joplin, I Got Dem
Ol' Kozmic Blues Again Mama!,
Columbia. 12" record cover, 1969.

25   Big Brother & The Holding
      Company, Cheap Thrills,
Columbia. 12" record cover, 1968.

26 Onward!! with R. Crumb
and His Cheap-Suit Serenaders,
promotional flyer, 1994.

27 The artwork of the flyer
with different bottomlines was
also used as a concert poster.

28 Ukelele Ike,
"I'm a Bear in a Lady's Boudoir",
Yazoo. 12" record cover, 1974.

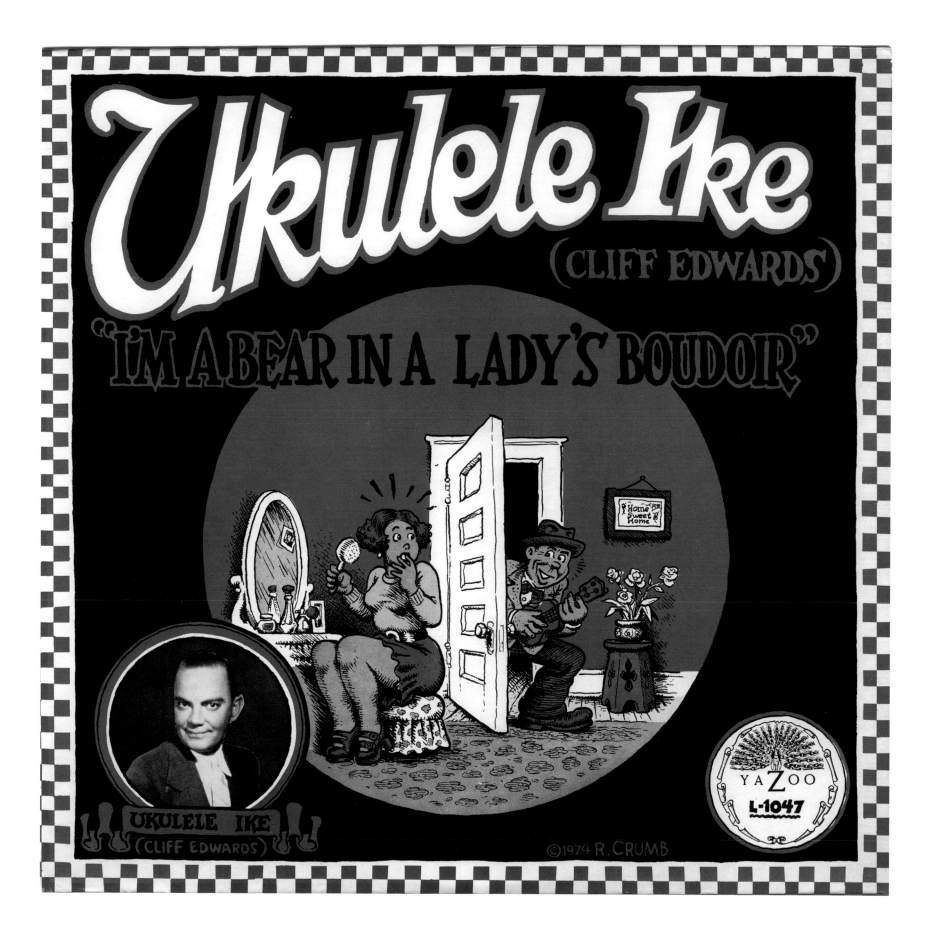

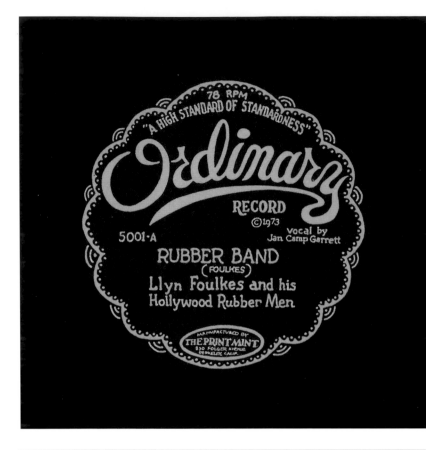

29 Ordinary Record,
drawing for a record label,
never published, 1973.

30 Big John Wrencher and His
Maxwell Street Blues Boys, Maxwell
Street Alley Blues, Barrelhouse.
12" record cover backside, 1974.

31 Ordinary Record,
drawing for a record cover,
never published, 1973.

32 Big John Wrencher and His
Maxwell Street Blues Boys, Maxwell
Street Alley Blues, Barrelhouse.
12" record cover, 1974.

35 R. Crumb & His DeLuxe String Orchestra, poster for a concert, 1974.

33 Sleeve design for Ordinary Record,
printed on brown paper, 1973.

36 The Hokum Boys, "You
Can't Get Enough of That Stuff",
Yazoo. 12" record cover, 1975.

34 Blue Goose Records, drawing for the
catalogue cover of a record company, 1975.

37 Eddie Lang,
Jazz Guitar Virtuoso, Yazoo.
12" record cover, 1978.

38 Advertisement in the catalogue
of Blue Goose Records for the first
album of R. Crumb and His Cheap
Suit Serenaders, 1975.

39 Blind Boy Fuller,
Truckin' My Blues Away, Yazoo.
12" record cover, 1978.

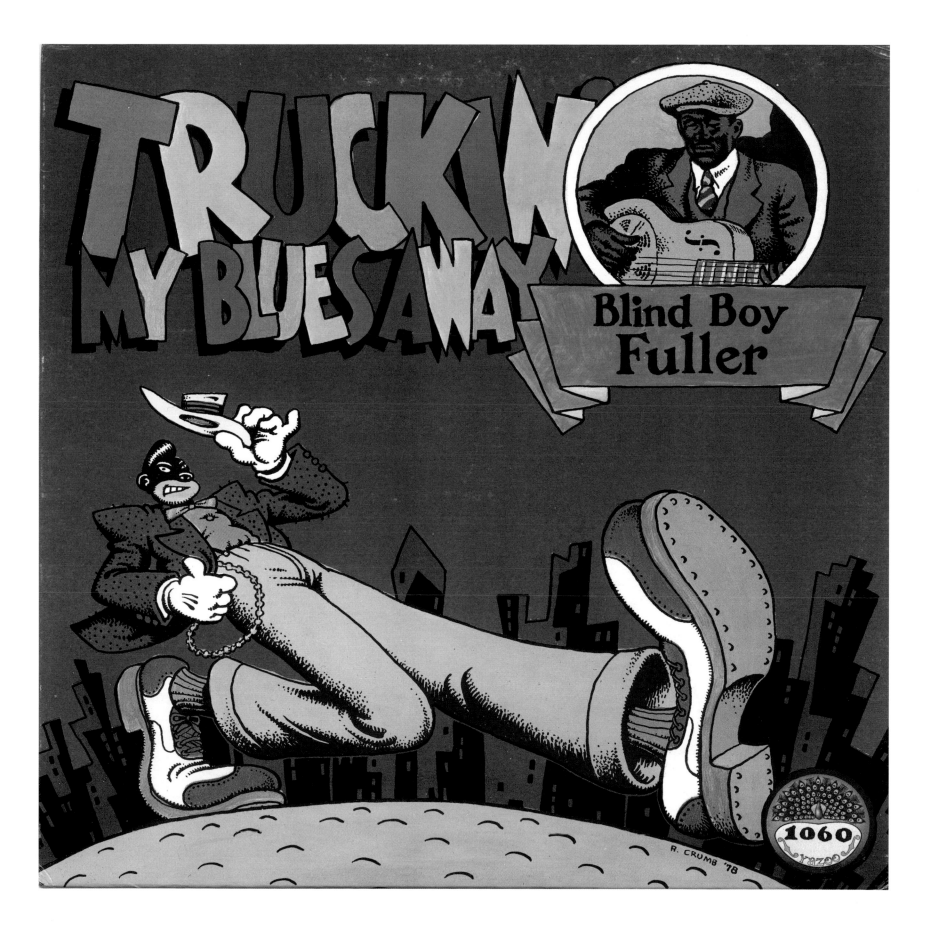

The CHEAP-SUIT SERENADERS "givin' 'em what they want" at a recent New Year's party

40 R. Crumb and His Cheap
Suit Serenaders, Blue Goose.
12" record cover backside, 1974.

41 R. Crumb and His Cheap
Suit Serenaders, Blue Goose.
12" record cover, 1974.

42 R. Crumb and His
Cheap Suit Serenaders,
Number Two, Blue Goose. 12"
record cover backside, 1976.

43 It's Old Home Week with
R. Crumb and His Cheap Suit
Serenaders, Blue Goose Records
advertisement, 1974.

44 Drawing in the booklet of the CD publication
of R. Crumb and His Cheap Suit Serenaders,
Number Two. Originally made, with another text
in the balloon, for Shanachie Records, 1975.

45 R. Crumb and His
Cheap Suit Serenaders,
Number Two, Blue Goose.
12" record cover, 1976.

46   R. Crumb and The Cheap Suit
Serenaders, Number Three, Blue Goose.
12" record cover backside, 1978.

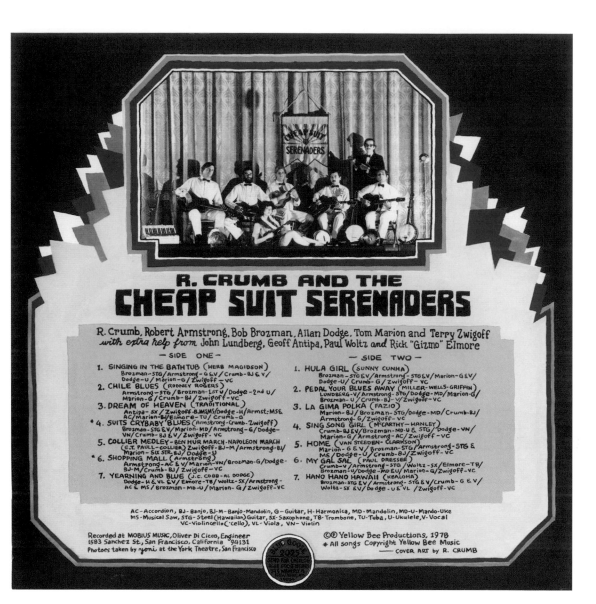

47   Blue Goose Records, drawing for a
catalogue cover of a record company, 1978.

48   R. Crumb and The Cheap Suit
Serenaders, Number Three, Blue Goose.
12" record cover, 1978.

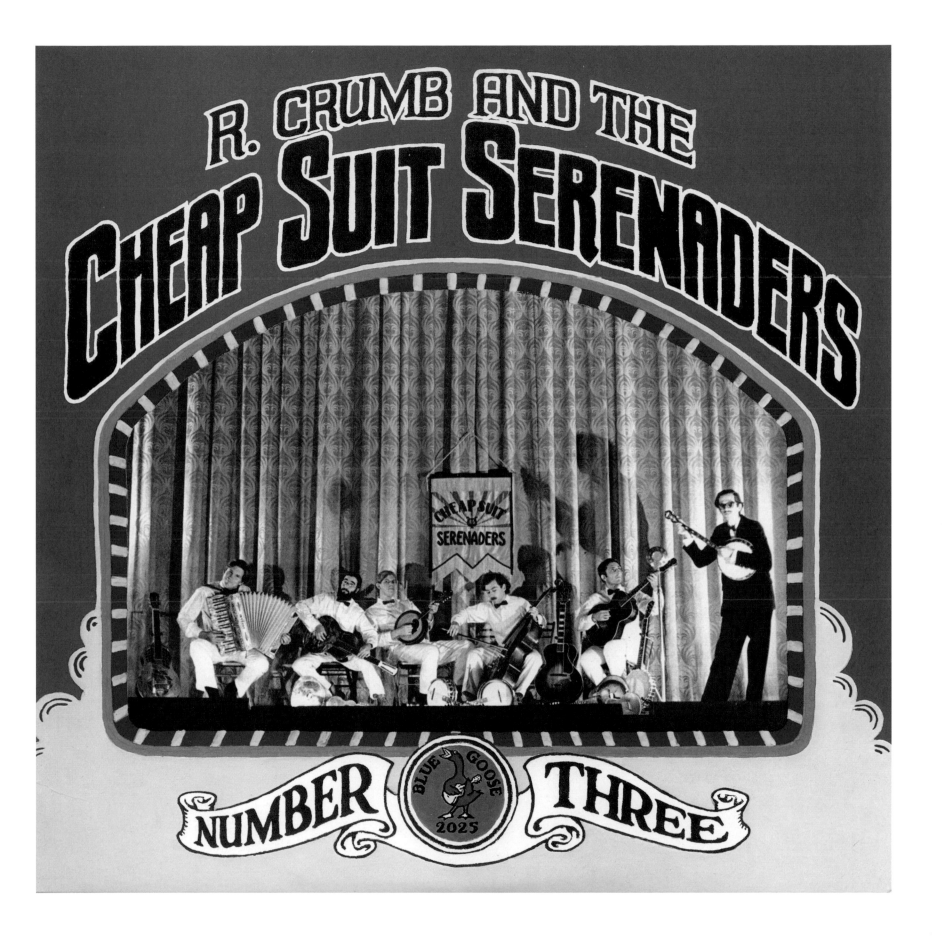

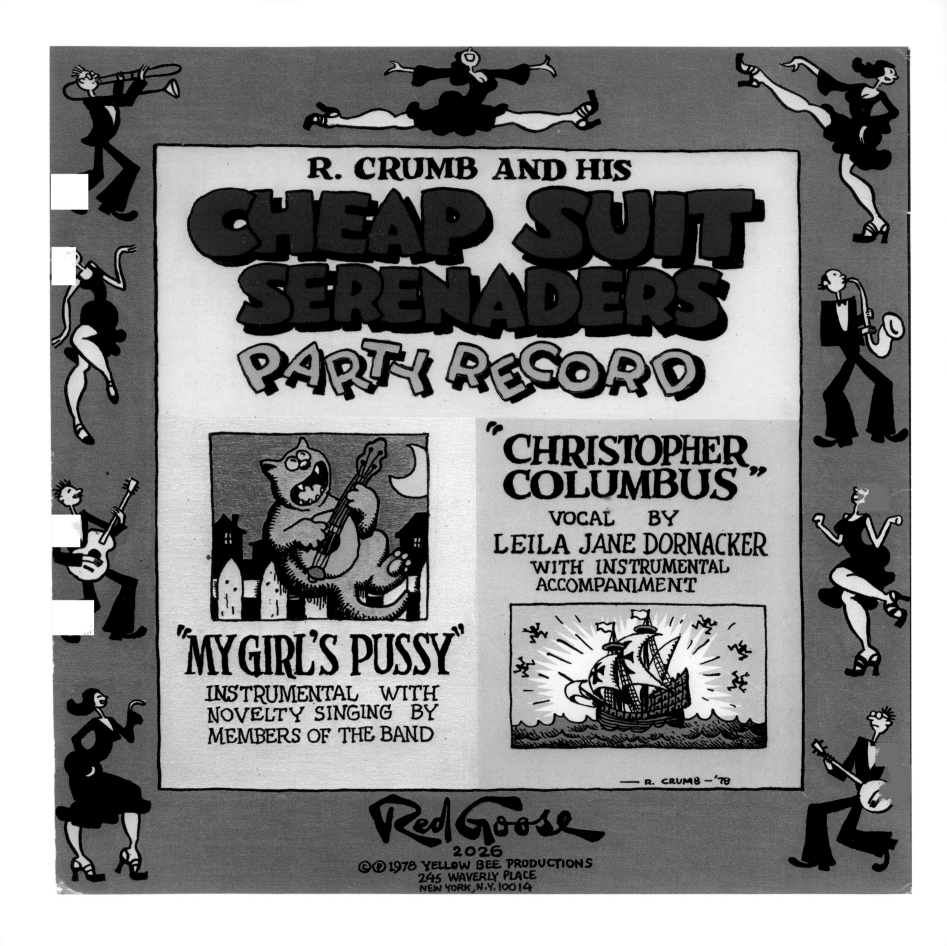

51   WayHi, drawing for a logo of
a music cassette company, 1990.

52   Charley's Choice, sticker
for a record-collector, 1977.

50   R. Crumb and The Cheap Suit
Serenaders, Party Record, Blue Goose.
12" record cover, 1978.

49   R. Crumb and His Cheap Suit
Serenaders, Party Record, Blue Goose.
12" record cover backside, 1978.

55   Bo Carter,
Banana in Your Fruit Basket,
Red Hot Blues 1931-36, Yazoo.
12" record cover, 1978.

53   It's Hot Stuff!!, R. Crumb and His Cheap
Suit Serenaders, promotional flyer, 1974.

54   Just Plain Folk, modified version of It's Hot
Stuff!! Lettering clearly not by R. Crumb, 1974.

57   Casey Bill Weldon and Kokomo Arnold,
Bottleneck Guitar Trendsetters of the 1930s,
Yazoo. 12" record cover, 1975.
The green colors of the original design
were modified by the publisher.

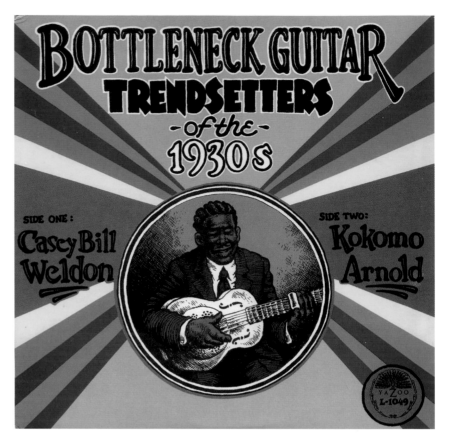

56   The Lighting Express No. 3 1976,
Arhoolie Record, magazine cover, 1974.

58   A.B. Riffle, portrait, 1975.

59   Roy Smeck plays Hawaiian Guitar,
Banjo, Ukelele and Guitar, 1926-1949, Yazoo.
12" record cover, 1975.

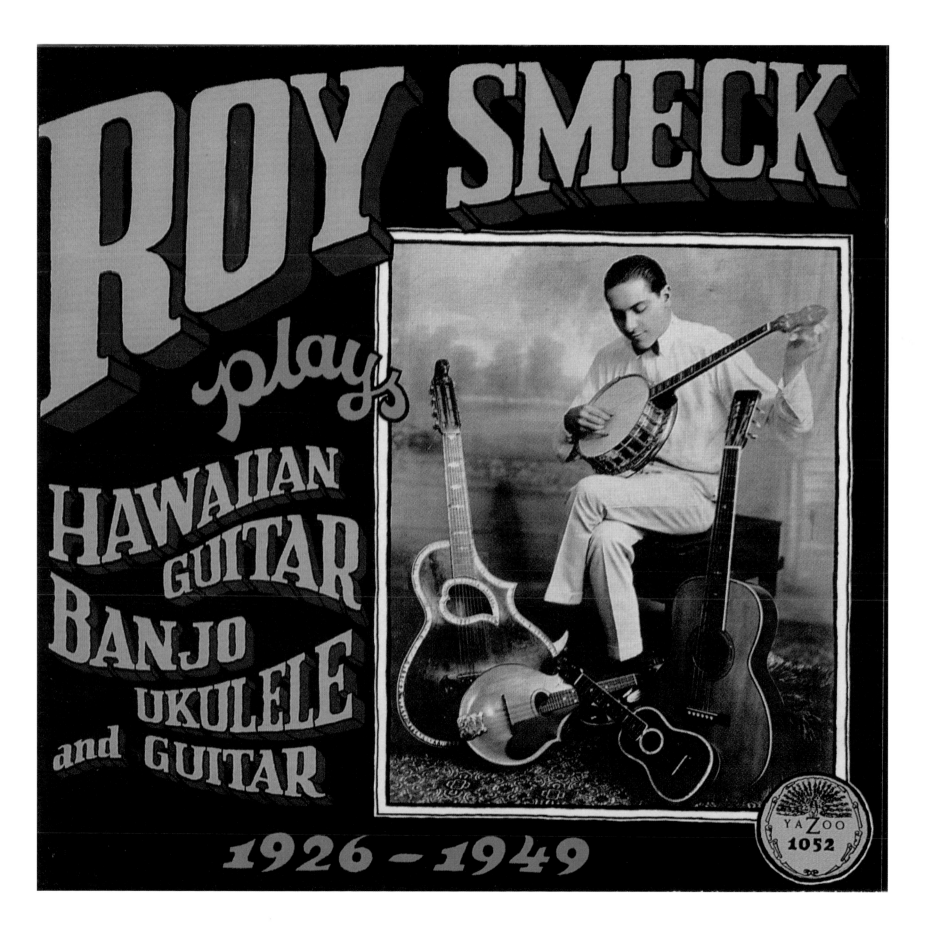

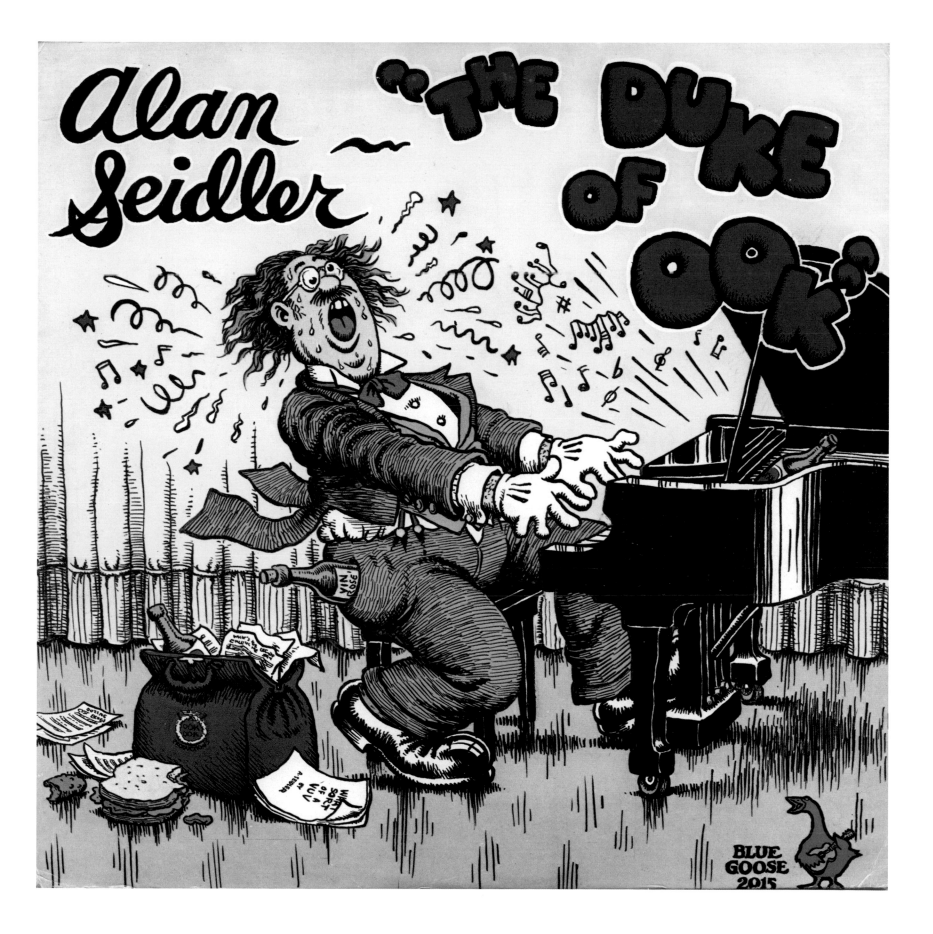

60 Superbatone, record label, 1989.

61 Morning Star Records, record label, 1980.

62 Blue Goose, record label, 1975.

63 Red Goose, record label, 1978.

64 Alan Seidler, The Duke of Ook, Blue Goose. 12" record cover, 1974.

65 Memphis Jug Band, Double Album, Yazoo. 12" record cover backside, 1979.

66 Yazoo Records, drawing for a catalogue cover of a record company, 1976.

67 Memphis Jug Band, Double Album, Yazoo. 12" record cover, 1979.

68 Yazoo's History of Jazz, various artists, Yazoo. 12" record cover backside, 1979.

69 Yazoo Records drawing for catalogue cover of a record company, 1976.

70 Yazoo's History of Jazz, various artists, Yazoo. 12" record cover, 1979.

Carolina Shout (1944)
featuring: James P. Johnson, piano.

Monday Date (1928)
featuring: Jimmy Noone, clarinet; Earl Hines, piano.

Night Life (1930)
featuring: Mary Lou Williams, piano.

Chimes Blues (1923)
featuring: Joe "King" Oliver, cornet; Louis Armstrong, cornet; Johnny Dodds, clarinet; Lil Hardin, piano.

Stomp Time Blues (1927)
featuring: Freddie Keppard, cornet; Johnny Dodds, clarinet; Tiny Parham, piano.

Chicago Buzz (1926)
featuring: Junie Cobb, clarinet; Johnny Dodds, clarinet; Jimmy Blythe, piano.

Jazz Battle (1929)
featuring: Jabbo Smith, cornet; Ikey Robinson, banjo.

Parkway Stomp (1928)
featuring: Ernest "Punch" Miller, cornet; Alex Hill, piano.

That's A Plenty (1940)
featuring: Muggsy Spanier, cornet; Sidney Bechet, clarinet.

Hay Foot, Straw Foot (1925)
featuring: Coleman Hawkins, clarinet/tenor sax/bass sax; Fletcher Henderson, piano.

Kansas City Shuffle (1926)
featuring: Lammar Wright, cornet; Bennie Moten, piano.

Clementine (1927)
featuring: Bix Beiderbecke, cornet; Frank Trumbauer, C-melody sax; Joe Venuti, violin; Eddie Lang, guitar; Steve Brown, string bass.

Sweet Peter (1929)
featuring: Jelly Roll Morton, piano; "Pops" Foster, string bass.

Fast and Furious (1932)
featuring: Duke Ellington, piano.

Muskrat Ramble (1929)
featuring: Joe "Wingy" Mannone, trumpet; Benny Goodman, clarinet.

Lookin' Good But Feelin' Bad (1929)
featuring: Thomas "Fats" Waller, piano; Jack Teagarden, trombone.

"Jazz started in New Orleans." So said Ferdinand Le Menthe, better known as Jelly Roll Morton, who spent the rest of his life enriching ours through his extraordinary creativity as a jazz soloist, composer, arranger and leader of the Red Hot Peppers, a studio jazz band known for its perfect performances on records. Because New Orleans was the only city in the United States with a tradition of holding parades for all occasions, the marching bands got plenty of practice the year round. These bands vied for the position of being the first band starting each parade, with the cornetist assuming leadership at the beginning of the parade. He was given the title of "King". This album presents the three "Kings" of New Orleans jazz—Freddie Keppard (1889-1933), Joe Oliver (1885-1938) and his protege, Louis Armstrong (1900-1971). New Orleans spawned such other jazz masters on this album as trumpeters Punch Miller and Wingy Mannone, string bassist, Pops Foster, and clarinetists Johnny Dodds, Jimmie Noone, Sidney Bechet and Omer Simeon. Because musicians were a dime-a-dozen in that musically overpopulated town, jazzmen moved to the largest city in the midwest—Chicago—where they found ample opportunities to perform due to wide public acceptance.

Although only two of our jazzmen were born in this city (Muggsy Spanier and Benny Goodman), Chicago became the center of jazz throughout the 20's. Musicians (especially from the midwest) gravitated to Chicago where the recording companies had their studios. Both Bennie Moten and Tiny Parham grew up in Kansas City, but worked their way to Chicago. Bix Beiderbecke from Davenport, Iowa; Jimmy Blythe from Louisville, Kentucky; Coleman Hawkins from St. Joseph, Missouri all found employment in this bountiful town.

As jazz picked up momentum in the early 20's, the deep South contributed such major recording artists as Fletcher Henderson, Jabbo Smith, Mary Lou Williams, Lammar Wright, Alex Hill, Junie Cobb, Ikey Robinson and Lil Hardin. The East Coast, too, gave of its plenty with James P. Johnson, Fats Waller, Earl Hines, Duke Ellington, Joe Venuti and Eddie Lang.

The earliest jazz bands consisted of five instruments: cornet, trombone, clarinet, piano and drums, playing together in an improvised manner. As the alto saxophone gained in popularity by 1920, it, along with the four-string banjo was added. As the 20's progressed, the jazz band grew larger (eventually reaching from twelve to fourteen pieces), expanding by doubling, tripling and even quadrupling trumpets, trombones and the reeds—clarinets and saxophones. When this happened an arranger was necessary to write out each part so that there wouldn't be any clashing of ideas.

Because disc recording was available at the creation of this excitingly new popular American music, not only could the tunes be preserved for the future, but so could the collective sound of the individual bands playing, along with their unique characteristics. Additionally the immediate creativity of the band members in relating musically to one another could be made permanent on record. The balance and individual relationships forming the overall sound of the band varied from group to group. Never was recording more important in the maintenance of the sound of the particular bands when they were fresh and contemporary. Because some of these bands were more influential than others, the way they played their tunes as exemplified on disc was handed down from one generation to another.

The basic do-it-yourself instrument was the piano which dealt simultaneously with the three basic ingredients of jazz: melody, harmony and rhythm. It was no wonder that the first musical impulse of the jazz band came from piano ragtime. As the jazz bands played for dancing, they included the blues and pop tunes of the day in their repertoire. Ultimately the most lasting contributions were created by the leaders who wrote original tunes for themselves and their groups.

This album has it all and features the most important jazzmen of their time. Yazoo has attempted in this LP to bring you the performances of the artists depicted on "Early Jazz Greats" trading cards. We managed to get 34 out of 36 artists on this LP. A set of "Early Jazz Greats" trading cards can be obtained by writing to Yazoo.

YAZOO RECORDS INC.
245 Waverly Place
New York, N.Y. 10014

Cover & back art: R. Crumb
Notes: David Jasen
Mastering: Nick Perls

SEND FOR A FREE CATALOGUE
ALL YAZOO LP'S ARE AVAILABLE BY WRITING TO YAZOO RECORDS, INC.

Produced for Yazoo Records, Inc. by David Jasen & Nick Perls.

We wish to thank Terry Zwigoff and Sherwin Dunner for their cooperation with this project.

We wish to thank Bob Altshuler, Dan Goetter, Charlie Huber, Dave Jasen, Nick Perls, & Dick Spottswood for the loan of their rare originals.

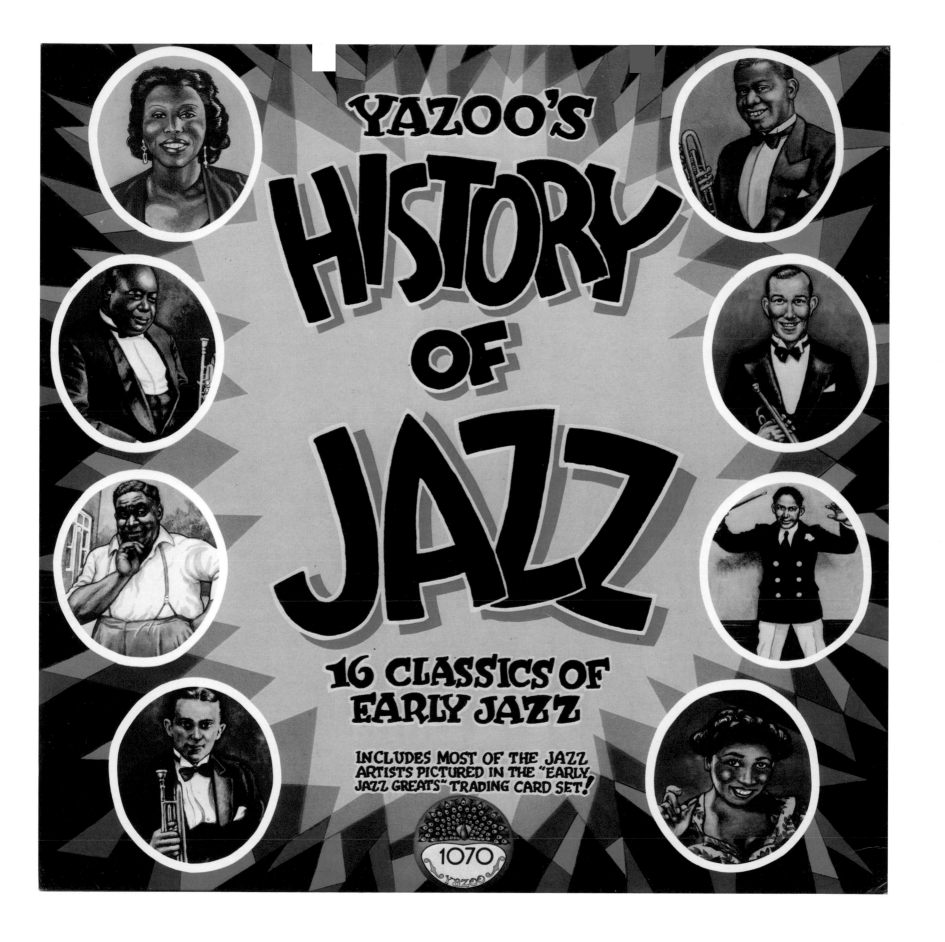

71   San Francisco Jazz
on Flexo 1930 to '32,
various artists, Echo.
12" record cover, 1987.

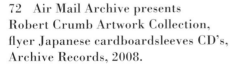

72   Air Mail Archive presents
Robert Crumb Artwork Collection,
flyer Japanese cardboardsleeves CD's,
Archive Records, 2008.

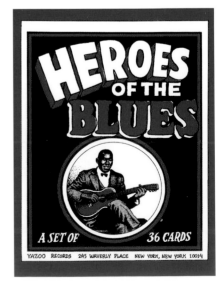

73   Heroes of the Blues
box for 36 trading cards,
frontside. Yazoo, 1978.

74   Heroes of the Blues. publicity poster for a box with 36 trading cards, Denis Kitchen Publ. reprint, 2005.

WILD FAMILY ORCHESTRA
from ZAMORA, CALIFORNIA

FRED - TRUMPET
HAROLD - BANJO, GUITAR & VOCALS
EVA - PIANO
MARGARET - DRUMS
CLAUDE - VIOLIN

— SIDE ONE —

1. RIENZI TWO-STEP
2. LITTLE OLD RAG DOLL
   M.M. COLE PUBLISHING CO.
3. JOHNNY MIND YOUR MAMMY
   M.M. COLE PUBLISHING CO.
4. WHERE THE RIVER SHANNON FLOWS
   WARNER BROS. INC. (ASCAP)
5. SOUTHERN BELLES MARCH
6. ZIG ZAG WALTZ
7. ARLINGTON HORNPIPE
   M.M. COLE PUBLISHING CO.
8. YELLOW ROSE OF TEXAS
   M.M. COLE PUBLISHING CO.

— SIDE TWO —

1. PRIZE WALTZ
   T.B. HARMS CO. (ASCAP)
2. SAN ANTONIO ROSE
   IRVING BERLIN MUSIC CORP. (ASCAP)
3. HAWTHORNE WALTZ
4. SUMMER DAYS SCHOTTISCHE
5. NOBODY'S DARLING BUT MINE
   SOUTHERN MUSIC PUBLISHING CO. (ASCAP)
6. EVERGREEN SCHOTTISCHE
7. IN THE MOOD
   SHAPIRO, BERNSTEIN & CO. (ASCAP)
8. HEEL AND TOE POLKA
9. THE WALTZ YOU SAVED FOR ME
   LEO FEIST INC. (ASCAP)

ALL SONGS RECORDED LIVE AT THE WILD FAMILY'S HOME - SUMMER, 1979

The Wild Family in the late 'Thirties: Claude, Margaret, Forrest, Grandmother, Harold, Eva, Fred, and Fred Sr.

Harold, Claude and Fred during World War II

The Wild Family Orchestra has been playing music in Yolo County, California since the early 'Thirties. Their father, Fred Wild Sr. owned and operated the General Store in Zamora and inspired his children by playing trumpet, fiddle, accordion, harmonica, and other instruments. As a family orchestra the Wilds played for many a Saturday night dance, as well as parties, picnics, and weddings. Fred Sr. passed away in 1949, but the five children kept the band going. Another brother, Forrest, who played Saxophone, died in 1940 from a mosquito bite. Today the Wilds still play together in the fine, old-time traditional style and run the family farm as they have since 1931.

— ALINE KOMINSKY-CRUMB

The Wild's Grandmother and Fred Sr. in the old Zamora General Store, which he operated. Taken in 1932.

Fred Sr. in his younger days

Zamora Union School Orchestra, Claude Wild, 2nd from left. May 17th, 1935

THANKS FOR TECHNICAL ASSISTANCE FROM GREGG GANNON, WALLY SUMM, AND NICK PERLS, AND FOR LEGAL ASSISTANCE FROM JANE LYNCH. COVER ART BY R. CRUMB

Fred with his trumpet, in the Army during World War II.

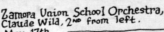

The Wilds' mother, Katie

YOLO RECORD 001

PHOTO BY HAL EMISON

76 Wild Family Orchestra from Zamora,
California, Yolo Record. 12" record cover, 1979.

77 Yolo Record, record label, 1979.

78 Shanachie, record label, 1975.

Side One   001

WILD FAMILY ORCHESTRA

RIENZI TWO-STEP (Hazel)
LITTLE OLD RAG DOLL (Hamblin)
JOHNNY MIND YOUR MAMMY (Shaeffer)
WHERE THE RIVER SHANNON FLOWS (Russell)
SOUTHERN BELLES MARCH (Hazel)
ZIG ZAG WALTZ (Hazel)
ARLINGTON HORNPIPE (Shaeffer)
YELLOW ROSE OF TEXAS
    (Arr. by Manoloff)
Copyright © 1979 Wild Family

75 Wild Family Orchestra from Zamora,
California, Yolo Record. 12" record cover
backside, 1979.

79 King of the Delta Blues, The Life and Music of Charlie Patton, by Stephen Calt and Gayle Wardlow, Yazoo. Publicity for a book with the image of the cover, 1987. In a modified version it appeared on a Yazoo CD with the same title.

81 "Hell Hound On My Trail", Robert Johnson drawing for silkscreen, Alex Wood, 1990.

80 78 Quarterly Volume 1 Number 4, published by Pete Whelan, magazine cover, 1988.

82 Dave Jasen, Rompin' Stompin' Ragtime, Blue Goose. 12" record cover, 1974.

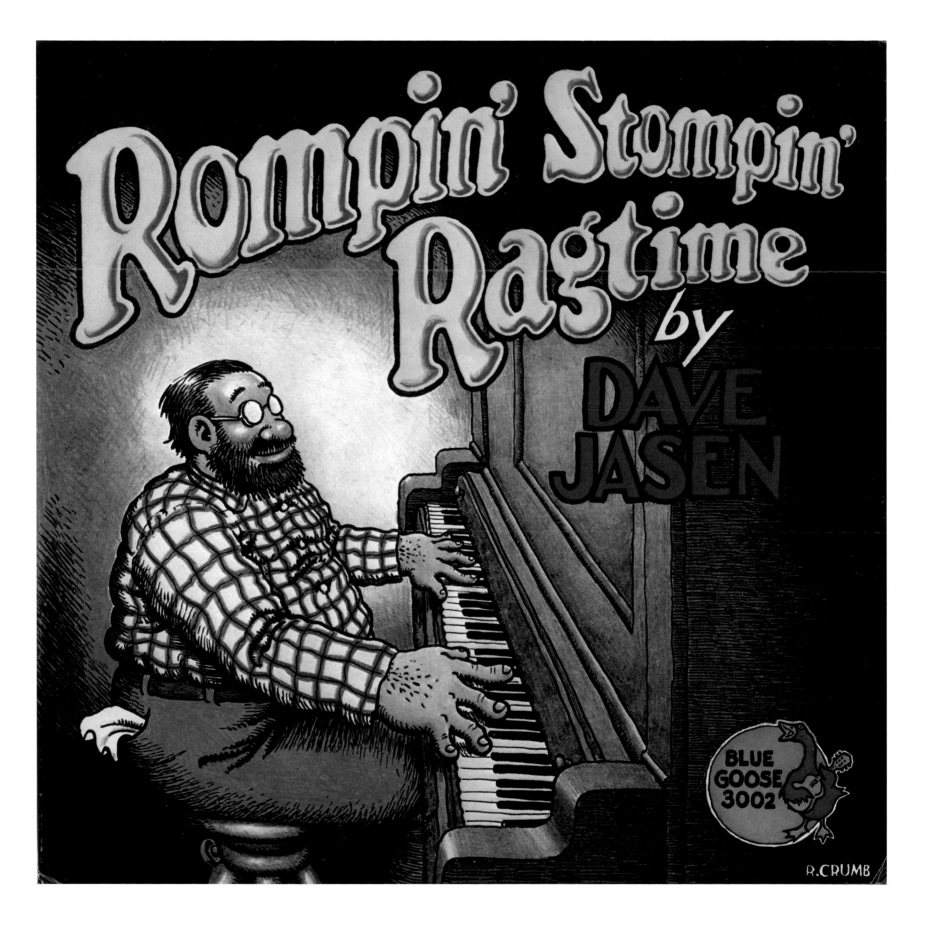

83 R. Crumb's Heroes of Blues, Jazz & Country, book cover, Abrams, 2005.

84 L'Argot des Musiciens, Didier Roussin, Madeleine Juteau, Alain Bouchaux, Editions Climats. Book cover, 1992. Besides the cover, this dictionary has 21 illustrations by R. Crumb.

85 Professor Gizmo, calling card, 1979.

86 Possum Trot String Band, calling card, 1979.

87 Wally Summ Music Studio, calling card, 1979.

ART BY R. CRUMB, 1980

92 Louie Bluie,
Arhoolie Records.
12" record cover, 1985.

89 Me And Big Joe,
illustration for article
by Michael Bloomfield,
High Times #64, 1980.

90 Portraits of blues musicians
for the article "Me and Big Joe"
by Michael Bloomfield, High
Times #64, 1980.

Tampa Red   Kokomo Arnold   Jazz Gillum   Tommy McClennan

91 Me And Big Joe,
illustration for article
by Michael Bloomfield,
High Times #64, 1980.

94   Gert Jan Blom, founder of the Beau Hunks Orchestra, 1995. Used on the CD booklet cover "Liedjes van Ordelijke ellende", Basta, 2004.

93   LeRoy Shield, portrait of the composer, for the CD booklet cover of "The Beau Hunks Play the Original Laurel & Hardy Music", Movies Select Audio 1993.

95   Gérard Dôle, CoCoColinda, Playa Sound. CD booklet cover, 1991.

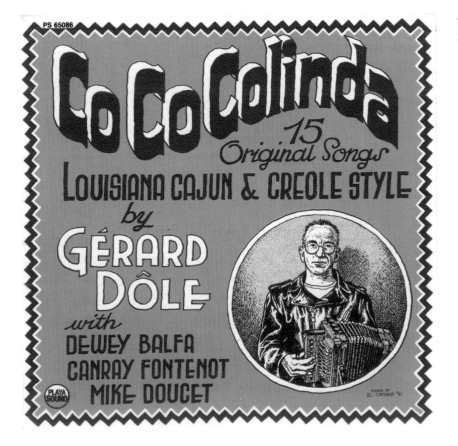

96   This modified version of the portrait of LeRoy Shield was published in the booklet of "The Beau Hunks Play The Original Laurel & Hardy Music Volume 2", Movies Select Audio, 1993.

97   The Klezmorim, Streets of Gold, Arhoolie Records. 12" record cover, 1978.

98 Calling card (reverse side) for J.B. Rund, 1980.

99 Portrait of Gus Cannon, "Banjo Joe", 1985.

100 Alain Weill, portrait of the writer, collector and singer, 1976.

101 Pioneers of Country Music. Publicity poster for a box with 36 trading cards, Denis Kitchen Publ. reprint, 2005.

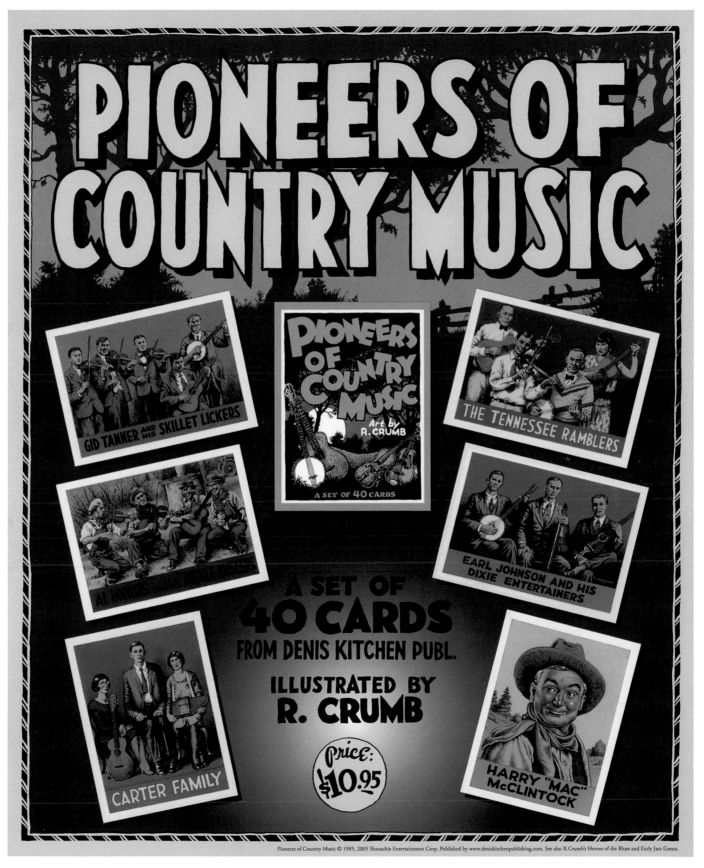

105   Les Primitifs du
Futur, Cocktail
d'Amour, Media Sept.
10" record cover, 1987.

103   Car City Records, design for
a record store (with J.B. Rund as a
partner) in a Detroit suburb, 1980.

102   Les Primitifs du Futur, Suivi de
Bluestory & the New Blue 4, Paris Jazz
Corner Productions, CD cover, 2000.

104   Cocktail d'Amour, Paris Jazz
Corner Productions, CD label, 2001.

106 Les As de Musette,
box for 36 trading cards,
Oog & Blik, 1994.

108 Paris Musette au Faubourg,
poster for a concert, 1992.

107 Bras et Garrigoux, notes
for Portfolio Les As de Musette,
Les Fréres Lumineux, 2002.

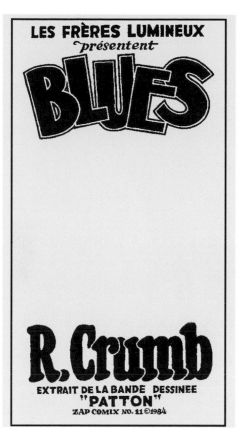

109   Blues R. Crumb, portfolio, Zap nr.11,
1984, Les Frères Lumineux, 2002.

110   Gus Viseur a Bruxelles,
Accordeon Magazine, 2000.

111   Espoir Perdu, portrait, 1994.

113 Diane Tell, Marilyn Montreuil, Columbia, 1991. As it was published on the inlay of the music cassette and the bottom inlay of the CD.

112 KC6WQJ, Dorrick & Marsha Minnis, drawing for a logo of a radio station, 1991.

114 Diane Tell, Marilyn Montreuil, Columbia. 7" record cover backside, 1991. This modified version of the drawing also appeared on a poster.

115 The Otis Brothers, Flying Crow, drawing for a LP, Universal Spider Productions, 1987.

James Brown
by R. Crumb
2000

James Brown
by R. Crumb
2000

Bo Diddley
by R. Crumb
2000

116   Portrait of James Brown,
The New Yorker, 2000.

117   Portrait of James Brown,
The New Yorker, 2000.

118   Portrait of Bo Diddley,
The New Yorker, 2000.

119   The Music Never Stopped, Roots of the
Grateful Dead, Shanachie. 12" record cover, 1995.

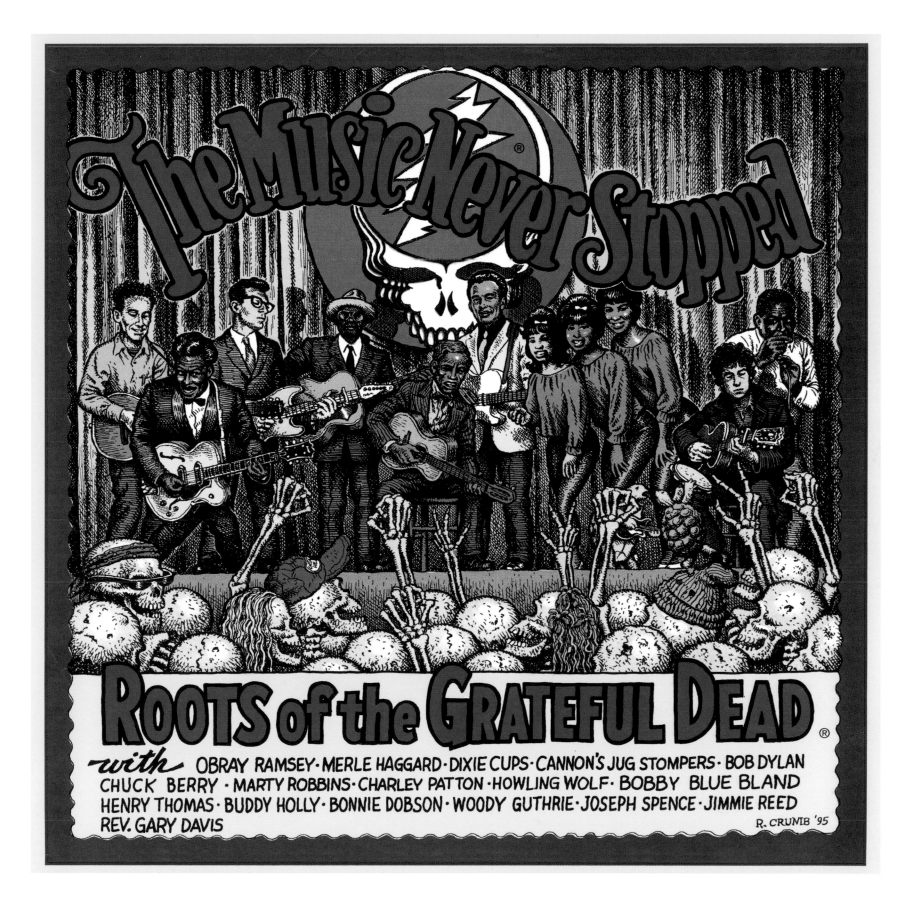

120 Portrait of
Frank Zappa for
The New Yorker,
1992.

121 I OWN 'EM,
record label for 10"
record made for luxe
edition Record Cover
Collection,
Oog & Blik, 1994.

122 Crumb, Original Soundtrack from the Terry
Zwigoff documentary, CD booklet cover, 1995.

123 Portrait of
Lightnin' Hopkins, 1974.

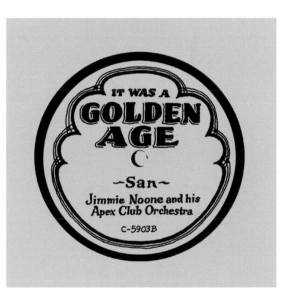

124   Paris Jazz Corner Productions,
        record label, 2000.

125   Low Life record label for
        Tony Boldin, 1996.

126   Fetish, record label, 1998.

127   Big Sport, Electric Records, 1996.

128   It Was a Golden Age, record label, 1996.

129   The Devil's Music, record label, 1996.

130   Paris Jazz Corner Productions,
        record label, 2000.

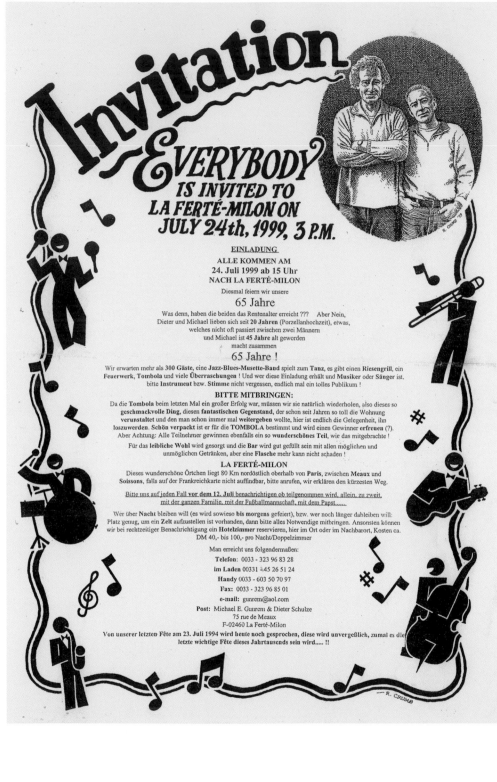

131 Invitation,
La Ferté-Milon, 1999.

132 Emile Vacher,
portrait, 1989.

133 Marceau,
portrait, 1990.

134 Woody Guthrie,
portrait, 1992.

135 George Jones,
portrait, 1993.

136 Emile Vacher,
portrait, 1993.

138 Les Primitifs du Futur, "Trop de Routes, Trop de Trains" et autres Histoires d'Amour, CD booklet cover, 1994.

137 Photo Robert Crumb and Dominique Gravic (1990), photo CD booklet Les Primitifs du Futur, World Musette, Sketch Studio, 1999.

140 Single d'Amour, CD label, Paris Jazz Corner Productions, 2005.

139 Les Primitifs du Futur, Single d'amour, drawing made in 1993, CD single, Paris Jazz Corner Productions, 2005.

141 Marie-Musette, illustration in the CD booklet of Trop de Routes, Trop de Trains et autres Histoires d'Amour, 1994.

142 La Femme Panthére et l'Homme Sandwich, illustration in the CD booklet of Trop de Routes, Trop de Trains et autres Histoires d'Amour, 1994.

143 La Belle et le Manouche, illustration in the CD booklet of Trop de Routes, Trop de Trains et autres Histoires d'Amour, 1994.

144 Pourvu Que Ça Mousse, drawing
for various publications of the band, 1992.

145 Dans Les Bayous de la Louisiane,
Gérard Dôle, 1997.

146 R. Morand Cajun Band.
After Pourvu Que Ça Mousse split up,
part of the drawing continued, 1992.

147 Acousteack, calling card, 1995.

148 Merle Haggard, illustration for The New Yorker, 1996.

MERLE HAGGARD

149 Singin' in the Bathtub, illustration originally done in 1987 as a promo for a bathroom supply warehouse in exchange for bathroom fixtures.

Amos Easton
KNOWN AS
"Bumble Bee Slim"

150   Festival de
Trompette, advertisement,
Sauve, France, 1996.

151   Amos Easton known as
"Bumble Bee Slim", silkscreen,
Cornélius, 1999.

152   Amos Easton known
as "Bumble Bee Slim",
portrait, 1997.

Amos Easton
KNOWN AS
"Bumble Bee Slim"

153   The Cheap Suit Serenaders, copied from
an old photograph, requested by Al Dodge
in exchange for some old 78 rpm records, 1995.

154   Bessie Smith and
Clarence Williams, portrait, 1997.

155   Bessie Smith,
Jazzman magazine, 2000.

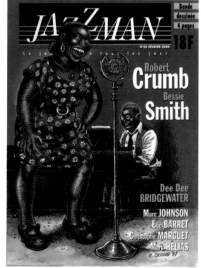

156   Bluestory, 1974-'75, '79 and
The New Blue 4, 1980, cover CD,
Paris Jazz Corner Productions, 1998.

157 Ian McCamy, friend
and fellow musican, 1999.

158 The Beau Hunks Saxophone Soc-
tette, Basta. CD booklet cover, 1999.

160   Fête du Tapage, silkscreen print for the portfolio Calendrier des Fêtes Oubliées, 1998.

159   R. Crumb and His Lil' Ol' Banjo, selfportrait, silkscreen, Cornélius, 1999.

161   Cover portfolio Calendrier des Fêtes Oubliées, 1998.

163 Portrait of
Lud Gluskin, 1998.

162 Portrait of Ernie & Emilio Caceres,
Paris Jazz Corner Productions.
Picture disc, 1998.

164 Portrait of
Sam Wooding, 1998.

LUD
GLUSKIN
1929
by
R. CRUMB
1999

166   Portrait of
Lud Gluskin, 1999.

167   Portrait of Kansas Joe and
Memphis Minnie, for the portfolio
Beloved Music Makers of Days
Gone By, Alex Wood, 1999.

Kansas Joe
and
Memphis
Minnie

165   Paris Jazz Corner Productions, Ernie & Emilio Caceres,
Picture Disc, 1998.

170 North Carolina Ramblers, one of the three silkscreens for portfolio Beloved Music Makers of Days Gone By, Alex Wood, 1999.

168 Beloved Music Makers of Days Gone By set of 3 portraits, colophon for Portfolio, Alex Wood, 1999.

169 Certificate/Authenticity portfolio Beloved Music Makers of Days Gone By, Alex Wood, 1999.

171   Jack Teagarden, one of the three silkscreens for portfolio
Beloved Music Makers of Days Gone By, Alex Wood, 1999.

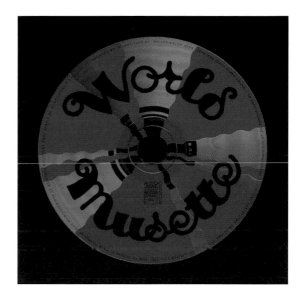

172   World Musette, CD label,
Sketch Studio, 1999.

173   Les Primitifs du Futur,
poster, 1999.

174   World Musette, poster, 1999.

175   Les Primitifs du Futur,
World Musette, CD cover, Sketch Studio, 1999.

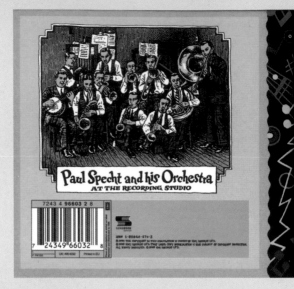

176   "That's What I Call
Sweet Music", CD cover and
booklet, EMI UK, 1999.

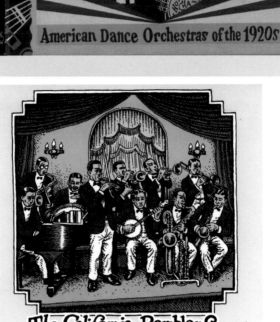

THE SEARCH FOR OLD MUSIC

"HAPPY DAYS AND LONELY NIGHTS" BY CHARLIE FRY AND HIS MIL-LION DOLLAR PIER ORCHESTRA—IT WAS A MOMENT OF REVELATION THE FIRST TIME I PLAYED THAT RECORD. I WAS 15 YEARS OLD; THE YEAR WAS 1959. I WAS AN ECCENTRIC KID, WOEFULLY OUT OF STEP WITH MY OWN TIME. I LIKED OLD THINGS. I WENT AROUND WEARING AN OLD ABE LINCOLN FROCK COAT. I *KIND OF* LIKED SOME OF THE EARLY ROCK AND ROLL RECORDS, BUT I *LOVED* THE BACKGROUND MUSIC IN THE OLD 1930S LAUREL & HARDY AND LITTLE RASCALS COMEDIES THAT I WATCHED ON T.V. KIDDIE SHOWS. I BOUGHT A FEW L.P.S AND 45S OF CURRENT DIXIELAND JAZZ AND RECREATIONS OF 'TWEN-TIES MUSIC, BUT THEY DIDN'T HAVE IT— SOME QUALITY I COULDN'T DEFINE. I'M STILL TRYING TO FIGURE IT ALL OUT. I WAS ALWAYS SNOOPING AROUND IN SECOND HAND STORES, LOOKING FOR OLD COMIC-BOOKS. ONE DAY I NOTICED SOME OLD 78 RECORDS WITH VERY INTRIG-UING LABELS. THEY RADIATED SOME KIND OF POWER- A MAGICAL AURA, EVEN THOUGH THE NAMES OF THE TUNES AND THE BANDS WERE UN-KNOWN TO ME. AT TEN CENTS APIECE, I BOUGHT A FEW OF THEM. TEN SECONDS AFTER PUTTING THE NEEDLE DOWN ON THAT CHARLIE FRY RE-CORD I KNEW—*THIS IS IT!* I WAS THRILLED TO THE CORE, OVER-JOYED! THIS WAS THE MUSIC I'D BEEN SEARCHING FOR! IT EXISTED ON OLD RECORDS! IN THAT MOMENT I BECAME A RECORD COLLECTOR FOR LIFE! FOUR DECADES HAVE PASSED AND I'M STILL AT IT, STILL SEARCH-ING, AND EVEN YET DISCOVERING OLD SHELLAC DISCS WITH OBSCURE, FORGOTTEN BYWAYS OF INCREDIBLE MUSIC HIDDEN IN THE GROOVES, SILENTLY WAITING FOR THE TURNTABLE TO MOVE, THE NEEDLE TO DROP. THERE'S A WEALTH OF GREAT MUSIC RECORDED IN THE '78 ERA, BEFORE THE ONSLAUGHT OF MASS MEDIA PROFOUNDLY CHANGED EVERYTHING... ...FOR EVER!

—R. CRUMB, AUGUST, 1998

Doc Cook & his 14 DOCTORS OF SYNCOPATION

"AT THE COLLEGE FRATERNITY DANCES AT MOST OF THE SMART EASTERN COLLEGES, THE WALTZ IS PRACTICALLY TABOO, WHICH IS A TRAGIC TREND TO ME BECAUSE I LOVE WALTZES, THEY ARE ONE OF MY BEST MEDIUMS OF EXPRES-SION. THEN THERE ARE THOSE WHO WANT ONLY 'HOT MUSIC; IF EVERYTHING IS NOT JAZZED UP, IT'S DULL AND BORING. THESE ARE USUALLY THE YOUNG FOLKS WHO HAVE HAD A FEW DRINKS. AND THEN, CONVERSELY, THERE ARE THOSE WHO LIKE THE SWEET, DREAMY MUSIC.

EITHER EXTREME IS BORING AND MONOTONOUS. THE CLE-VER ORCHESTRA LEADER IS HE WHO MAKES HIS PROGRAM UP OF A FEW SWEET SOFT TUNES, WITH OCCASIONAL VOCAL CHO-RUSES AMONG THE INSTRUMENTAL, FOLLOWED BY A WILD PEPPY TUNE, PLAYED EVER SO SOFTLY, BECAUSE 'PEP' IS NOT VOLUME AND LOUD RAUCOUS NOTES HAVE NEVER DELIGHTED THE EAR OF ANYONE.

I ONCE KNEW OF A DANCE HALL WHERE THE CLARINET WAS FORBIDDEN, DUE TO THE FACT THAT IT SEEMED TO HAVE A DEGENERATING EFFECT UPON THE DANCING OF A CERTAIN TYPE OF YOUNG PERSON WHO WENT THERE, ESPECIALLY WHEN IT WAS PLAYED IN ORIENTAL FASHION AGAINST TOM-TOM BEATS.

SO I AM FIRMLY CONVINCED THAT IT IS NOT THE VOLUME THAT MAKES FOR PEP BUT RATHER THE TYPE OF MUSIC AND THE STYLE OF THE RENDITION, AND I HAVE COME TO BELIEVE THAT A HAPPY MEDIUM IN LENGTH OF DANCE, SELECTION OF TUNES, VOLUME AND TEMPO WILL LEAD TO SUCCESS AS A DANCE ORCHESTRA DIRECTOR." —RUDY VALLEE

("VAGABOND DREAMS COME TRUE", AUTOBIOGRAPHY OF RUDY VALLEE, 1930)

SPECIAL THANKS TO: JOHN R.T. DAVIES, SUE DAVIES, TONY BALDWIN, RUTH EDGE AND LORA FOUNTAIN.

ALBUM COMPILED AND ILLUSTRATED BY: R. CRUMB.

PRODUCED BY: CIARA NOLAN.

ART DIRECTOR: MATT CURTIS @ AP;D.

VISIT THE WEBSITE - WWW. SONGBOOK-SERIES.CO.UK

177   La Ferté-Milon,
24 July '99, flyer, 1999.

179   Big Fun on the Bayou,
Gérard Dôle, CD cover, 1999.

178 Portrait of Michael and
Dieter, drawn in exchange for
old 78 rpm records, 1998.

180 Portrait of Hawks & Eagles
on CD booklet Songs From Days
Gone Bye, 1978/2003.

182 The Bal Musette, offprint,
Cornelius, France, 2000.

181 Dancing couple, offprint, 2004.

183   "Gay Life in Dikanka",
R. Crumb's Old-Time Favorites,
Bakhåll, Sweden, 2000.

184   "Gay Life in Dikanka",
R. Crumb's Old-Time Favorites,
inside illustration, Bakhåll, 2000.

185   "Gay Life in Dikanka",
R. Crumb's Old-Time Favorites,
playlist, Bakhåll, 2000.

186   "Gay Life in Dikanka",
R. Crumb's Old-Time
Favorites, text and
illustrations, Bakhåll, 2000.

188 Portrait of Artie Shaw, 2000.

187 "Kid Chocolat", illustration for the CD booklet of Les Primitifs Du Futur: "Trop de Routes, Trop de Trains", La Lichère, 1999.

189 Was Hast Du Für Gefühle Moritz?, CD booklet cover, Shimmy, 2000.

190 June Jam 2000, flyer, 2000.

191 Ménétrier Bressan, drawing from sketchbook, 2001.

192 Two women with hurdy-gurdys, 2001.

193 Musician with hurdy-gurdy, sketchbook, 2001.

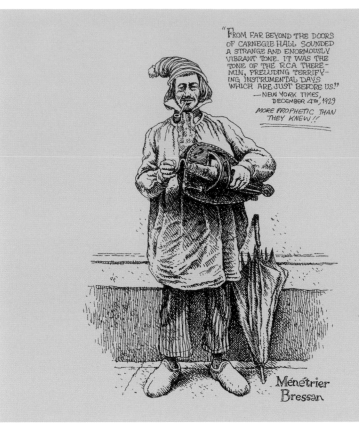

194   Bruno Priez Accordéons et
Plus, calling card, 2001.

195   Weems String
Band, 2001.

WEEMS STRING BAND

BACK BEFORE MANUFACTURED POP MUSIC WAS SHOVED DOWN OUR THROATS, WE HAD A
DIFFERENT KIND OF MUSICAL ENVIRONMENT. OUR ANCESTORS LIKED TO DANCE, AND THERE
WERE PLENTY OF MUSICIANS TO PROVIDE THE MUSIC. THESE MUSICIANS LEARNED TUNES FROM
THEIR SURROUNDINGS — RELATIVES, WANDERING MINSTRELS, LOCAL PLAYERS OF RENOWN.
THE WEEMS STRING BAND, FROM WESTERN TENNESSEE, WAS A FAMILY ORCHESTRA WHOSE ONE
78-R.P.M. RECORD, "DAVY/GREENBACK DOLLAR," IS A MAGNIFICENT EXAMPLE OF THIS LOST MUSIC.

196   Accordéons au Féminin,
CD cover, Paris Jazz Corner
Productions, 2000.

197   Les As du
Musette, Accordéons
au Féminin, Paris
Jazz Corner
Productions, 2000.

198 Musicians,
sketchbook, 2002.

199 Drawing from
sketchbook, 2002.

200 Hot Women, CD cover,
Kein & Aber Records, 2003.

201 Hot Women, CD label,
Kein & Aber Records, 2003.

202 La Niña de los Peines,
CD booklet for Hot Women,
Kein & Aber Records, 2003.

203 Yadana Muit,
CD booklet for Hot Women,
Kein & Aber Records, 2003.

204 Lidya Mendoza,
CD booklet for Hot Women,
Kein & Aber Records, 2003.

205 Rita Abadzi and Cleoma Falcon,
CD booklet for Hot Women,
Kein & Aber Records, 2003.

206 Leona Gabriel/Araci Cortes,
CD booklet for Hot Women,
Kein & Aber Records, 2003.

207 Cheikha Tetma,
CD booklet for Hot Women,
Kein & Aber Records, 2003.

209   Logo design for
record shop Sacramento,
California, 1999.

208   "The Drunken Landlady",
CD cover Ian McCamy,
Fremeaux & Associes, 2004.

210   "Sleep Sound in the Morning",
CD cover, Fremeaux & Associes, 1999.

211   Blues, R. Crumb, box for
portfolio Les Frères Lumineux, 2002.

212   Fiddlin' Ian McCamy and
his Celtic Reelers, CD back
cover,
Fremeaux & Associes, 2000.

213   B.B. King original
artwork for silkscreen,
unpublished, 2002.

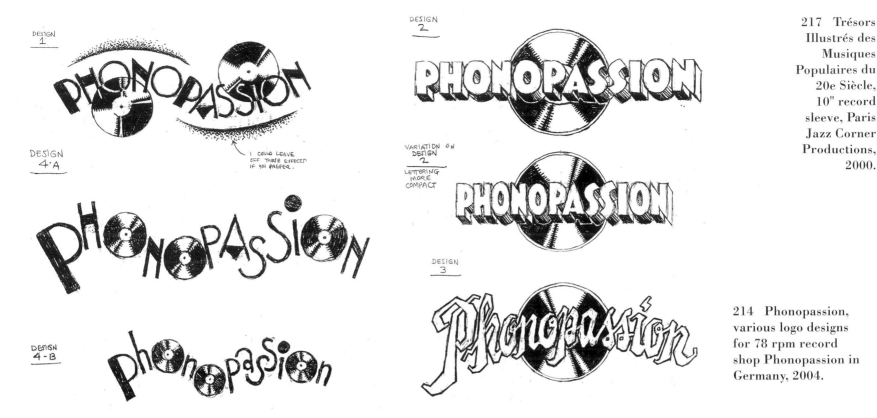

DESIGN 1

DESIGN 2

I COULD LEAVE OFF THESE EFFECTS IF YOU PREFER.

DESIGN 4·A

VARIATION ON DESIGN 2
LETTERING MORE COMPACT

217 Trésors Illustrés des Musiques Populaires du 20e Siècle, 10" record sleeve, Paris Jazz Corner Productions, 2000.

DESIGN 3

DESIGN 4·B

214 Phonopassion, various logo designs for 78 rpm record shop Phonopassion in Germany, 2004.

215 "Chimpin' the Blues", CD cover for radio program, 2003.

216 Does it get any better than this? sketchbook, 2003.

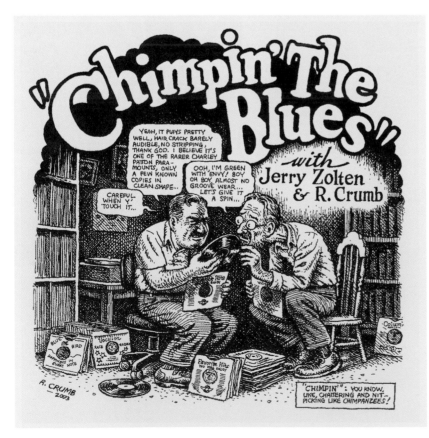

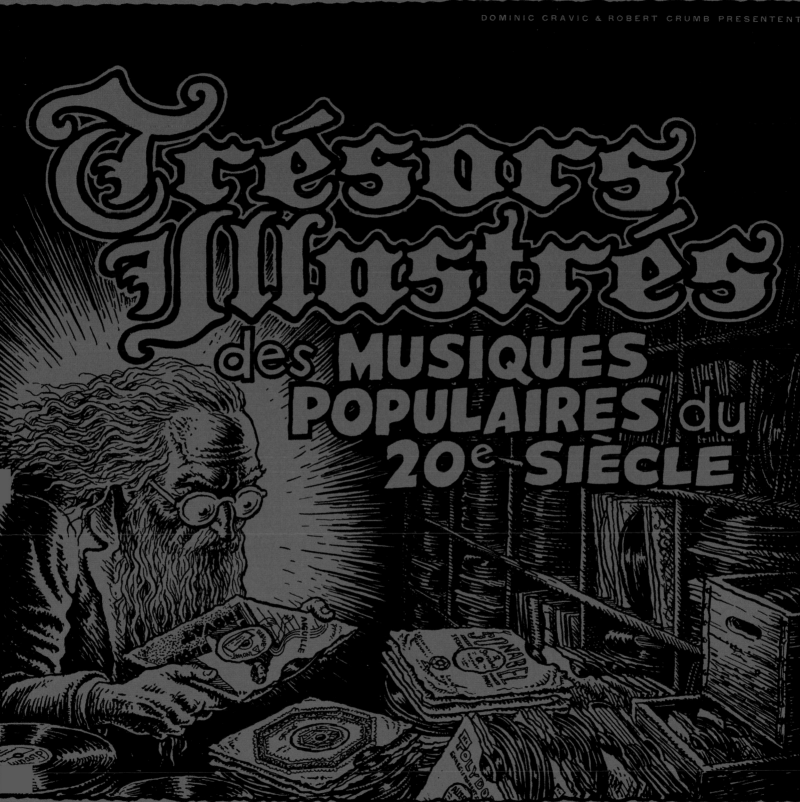

222 Schellack Rausch, portrait of two 78 rpm record collectors, 2005.

224 The Stuff That Dreams Are Made Of, cover of a 2-CD set, Yazoo, 2006.

223 Self portrait of R. Crumb opening a box with records, 2006.

218 Paris Jazz Corner Productions, 10" sleeve for Robert Johnson.

219 10" sleeves for 78 rpm records, Andrea Schmauder, Germany 2006.

220 10" sleeves for 78 rpm records, Andrea Schmauder, Germany 2006.

221 10" sleeves for 78 rpm records, Andrea Schmauder, Germany 2006.

225 Charlie Patton, BD Blues, Two CD's inserted in a book, Editions Nocturne, France, 2004.

PATTON

CHARLEY PATTON VÉCUT LA PLUS GRANDE PART DE SA VIE AU SEIN DES VASTES PLANTATIONS DOCKERY, DANS LES BASSES TERRES DU DELTA DU MISSISSIPI. C'ÉTAIT UN BON À RIEN PARESSEUX QUI VIVAIT AUX CROCHETS DES FEMMES ET PASSAIT LE PLUS CLAIR DE SON TEMPS DANS UNE TOTALE OISIVETÉ. C'ÉTAIT ÉGALEMENT UN GRAND INTERPRÈTE DONT ON SENT ENCORE AUJOURD'HUI L'INFLUENCE SUR LE BLUES ET LE ROCK, BIEN QUE PEU DE GENS AIENT ENTENDU PARLER DE LUI. LA MUSIQUE QU'IL CHANTAIT ET JOUAIT EST IMPOSSIBLE À DÉCRIRE. IL FAUT L'ÉCOUTER.

by R.Crumb 1984

POUR LES PAUVRES NOIRS QUI TRIMAIENT ET VIVAIENT ISOLÉS DANS CES PLANTATIONS, LE MODE DE VIE DIFFÉRAIT PEU DE CELUI DE L'ESCLAVAGE.

MAIS CHAQUE FERME, CHAQUE VILLE AVAIT SES MUSICIENS. DES CHANTEURS, DES GUITARISTES, DES VIOLONISTES, DES JOUEURS DE BANJO...

CHARLEY ÉTAIT ENCORE UN ADOLESCENT ET LE BLUES UN STYLE DE JEU NOUVEAU LORSQU'IL Y FUT INITIÉ AU DÉBUT DU SIÈCLE PAR UN MUSICIEN DE DOCKERY.

CET HOMME S'APPELAIT HENRY SLOAN.

HENRY SLOAN POURRAIT BIEN ÊTRE CE PIONNIER DU BLUES QUE W.C. HANDY ENTENDIT UN JOUR DE 1903 ALORS QU'IL ATTENDAIT UN TRAIN À TUTWILER, DANS LE MISSISSIPI.

MÊME LES NOIRS QUI ALLAIENT À L'ÉGLISE LE CONSIDÉRAIENT, LUI ET SES SEMBLABLES, COMME DE "MAUVAIS NÈGRES". LE BLUES ÉTAIT POUR EUX LA "MUSIQUE DU DIABLE".

À CETTE ÉPOQUE, IL JOUAIT DANS LES ENVIRONS AVEC LA FAMILLE CHATMON UN PETIT ENSEMBLE DE CORDES QUI INTERPRÉTAIT DU RAGTIME ET DES AIRS A LA MODE DANS LES SOIRÉES, LES PIQUE-NIQUES ET LES FÊTES.

MAIS MÊME CETTE MUSIQUE-LÀ ÉTAIT TROP INSIPIDE POUR LE JEUNE, INTENSE ET BOUILLONNANT PATTON. IL ÉTAIT IRRÉSISTIBLEMENT ATTIRÉ PAR LES RYTHMES PLUS COMPLEXES ET MOINS BLANCS D'HENRY SLOAN.

LE MEILLEUR AMI DE PATTON SEMBLE AVOIR ÉTÉ WILLIE BROWN. APRÈS AVOIR TRAÎNÉ DES ANNÉES AVEC CHARLEY, ÉTUDIANT SA MANIÈRE DE JOUER ET DE CHANTER, WILLIE BROWN DEVINT LUI-MÊME L'UN DES GRANDS DU BLUES DU DELTA.

ILS JOUAIENT PARFOIS EN-SEMBLE DANS DES BALS. WILLIE ASSURAIT LA RYTHMIQUE TAN-DIS QUE CHARLEY ENCHAÎNAIT LES TOURS POUR AMUSER LE PUBLIC. IL JETAIT SA GUITARE EN L'AIR, LA RATTRA-PAIT ENTRE SES JAMBES, ETC.

 LE BLUES GRAND PUBLIC ATTEIGNAIT PEU LES PAYSANS ISOLÉS DE LA RÉGION DU DELTA. LE VRAI BLUES, INCARNATION INTENSE ET DIRECTE DE LEUR EXISTENCE, Y POURSUIVAIT SON ÉVOLUTION. ET TOUS VENAIENT APPRENDRE AUPRÈS DE CHARLEY PATTON. IL ÉTAIT CONSIDÉRÉ COMME LE MEILLEUR, TANT PAR LES AUTRES MUSICIENS QUE PAR LES POULES DEVANT LESQUELLES IL JOUAIT.

IL SE SERVAIT DE SA VOIX COMME D'UN INSTRUMENT. IL CRIAIT, HURLAIT, BEUGLAIT ET GROGNAIT. IL TAPAIT SUR SA GUITARE, MARQUANT DES RYTHMES LOURDS PENDANT DE LONGS INTER-VALLES, PARFOIS JUSQU'À UNE DEMI-HEURE, TANDIS QUE LES GENS DANSAIENT.

PLUSIEURS DE SES CHANSONS PARLAIENT DE PARTIR, QUITTER UNE FEMME, VAGABONDER...

"JE M'EN VAIS, SWEET MAMA, TU VEUX PAS VENIR ? DIEU SEUL SAIT QUAND JE REVIENDRAI ICI!" (SCREAMIN' AND HOLLERIN' THE BLUES)

"UN DE CES JOURS, JE TE MANQUERAI, CHÉRIE, JE SAIS QUE JE TE MANQUERAI, FAIS DE BEAUX RÊVES, JE VAIS M'EN ALLER." (SOME OF THESE DAYS I'LL BE GONE)

MAIS SES CHANSONS PARLAIENT SURTOUT DE FAIRE LA NOCE : "J'AIME FAIRE DES HISTOIRES, SEIGNEUR, BOIRE COMME UN TROU DE LA CUVÉE SPÉCIALE ET TRAÎNER DANS LES RUES TOUTE LA NUIT." (ELDER GREEN BLUES)

VERS 1931, QUELQU'UN ESSAYA DE LUI TRANCHER LA GORGE, MAIS PATTON SURVÉCUT, GARDANT UNE VILAINE CICATRICE.

PATTON ÉTAIT CONNU POUR SON SALE CARACTÈRE ET SA "GRANDE GUEULE", CE QUI L'ENTRAÎNAIT SOUVENT DANS DES BAGARRES, ALORS QU'IL N'AVAIT PAS LA CARRURE POUR SE DÉFENDRE.

IL EST ÉGALEMENT BIEN ÉTABLI QU'IL SE BATTAIT VIOLEMMENT AVEC SES COMPAGNES. "SI LES BONNES FEMMES L'ÉNERVAIENT, IL LES FRAPPAIT, VOYEZ, IL LES COGNAIT AVEC SA VIEILLE GUITARE" RAPPORTE UNE ANCIENNE CONNAISSANCE.

À PARTIR DE 1930, PATTON VÉCUT AVEC UNE FEMME DU NOM DE BERTHA LEE, QUI FAISAIT LA CUISINE POUR LES FAMILLES BLANCHES DU VOISINAGE. LE COUPLE DÉMÉNAGEAIT ET SE DISPUTAIT SOUVENT PATTON LA RENDAIT RESPONSABLE DE SA SANTÉ DÉCLINANTE. IL L'ACCUSAIT DE L'AFFAMER. ILS SE SAOULAIENT ET S'ATTAQUAIENT L'UN L'AUTRE DANS DE VIOLENTS ACCÈS DE FUREUR.

AU MILIEU DES ANNÉES 20, UNE NOUVELLE GÉNÉRATION DE MUSICIENS DE BLUES ARRIVA EN FORCE DANS LE DELTA. PARMI EUX SE TROUVAIT UN ADOLESCENT NERVEUX APPELÉ ROBERT JOHNSON. IL VIVAIT PRÈS DE CHEZ WILLIE BROWN ET COMMENÇA À TRAÎNER DANS LE COIN, AFIN D'APPRENDRE LE BLUES AUPRÈS DE BROWN, PATTON ET SON HOUSE.

ENVIRON UN AN PLUS TARD, ROBERT JOHNSON REVINT ET LES ÉBLOUIT AVEC UN NOUVEAU STYLE DE BLUES UTILISANT UN RYTHME DE BASSE PUISSANT ET ENTRAÎNANT QU'IL AVAIT INVENTÉ TOUT SEUL. EN 1936 ET 1937, JOHNSON ENREGISTRA QUELQUES UNS DES MEILLEURS BLUES RURAUX DE TOUS LES TEMPS...

LOUISE JOHNSON ÉTAIT UNE JEUNE FILLE QUI JOUAIT UN BOOGIE WOOGIE MUSCLÉ DANS UN BAR DU COIN. PATTON ÉTAIT IMPRESSIONNÉ PAR SON JEU AUTANT QUE PAR SON ALLURE ET IL COMMENÇA À LUI FAIRE LA COUR.

SON HOUSE FUT UN AUTRE DES GRANDS CHANTEURS DU DELTA QUI FRÉQUENTA PATTON.
HOUSE VENAIT DE PASSER DEUX ANS À PARCHMAN, UNE FERME PÉNITENTIAIRE DU MISSISSIPI, POUR AVOIR TUÉ UN HOMME EN 1928, AU COURS D'UNE BAGARRE.
LA MUSIQUE DE SON HOUSE PLUT À PATTON, ET IL L'INVITA À LE SUIVRE EN COMPAGNIE DE WILLIE BROWN, POUR UNE SÉANCE D'ENREGISTREMENT À GRAFTON.

DES ANNÉES PLUS TARD, HOUSE SE VANTA DE LA FAÇON DONT IL AVAIT SOUFFLÉ LA PIANISTE À PATTON AU COURS DU VOYAGE.
"CHARLEY, IL ÉTAIT FURAX, ASSIS À L'AVANT. JE ME PENCHE VERS ELLE ET JE ME METS À LA BARATINER AUSSI SEC. "JE T'AIME VRAIMENT BIEN, TU SAIS" ET ON SE RESSERT UNE BONNE GORGÉE."

VERS 1930 LA SANTÉ DE PATTON SE DÉTÉRIORA SÉRIEUSEMENT. UNE VIE DURE ET DISSOLUE, PASSÉE À BOIRE DE L'ALCOOL DE MAÏS ET À FUMER CIGARETTE SUR CIGARETTE, COMMENÇAIT À PRODUIRE SON EFFET. IL ÉTAIT PROBABLEMENT DANS LA QUARANTAINE À CETTE ÉPOQUE.

SES CHANSONS PRIRENT ALORS UN TON PLUS INQUIÉTANT, PLUS DÉSESPÉRÉ. DANS "BIRD NEST BOUND", IL SEMBLE SOUPIRER APRÈS LA SÉCURITÉ ET LA STABILITÉ.
"SI J'ÉTAIS UN OISEAU, MAMA, J'ME TROUVERAIS UN NID AU CŒUR DE LA VILLE, ET QUAND LA VILLE ME RENDRAIT TROP SEUL, JE SERAIS UN OISEAU DANS SON NID."

OH HUSH   OH HUSH
SOMEBODY IS CALLING ME...

SES DERNIERS ENREGISTREMENTS MONTRENT QU'IL SE SAVAIT PROCHE DE LA FIN. "COMME LA LUNE A L'AIR JOLIE, BRILLANT PARMI LES ARBRES, JE VOIS BERTHA LEE, SEIGNEUR, MAIS ELLE NE ME VOIT PAS! (POOR ME)

BERTHA LEE ET LUI CHANTENT ENSEMBLE LA CHANSON "OH DEATH." ON Y ENTEND DE FAÇON SAISISSANTE LA PROXIMITÉ DE LA MORT ET L'HORREUR DE CHARLEY FACE À ELLE.

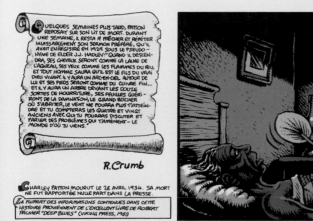

QUELQUES SEMAINES PLUS TARD, PATTON REPOSAIT SUR SON LIT DE MORT. DURANT UNE SEMAINE, IL RESTA À PRÊCHER ET RÉPÉTER INLASSABLEMENT SON SERMON PRÉFÉRÉ, QU'IL AVAIT ENREGISTRÉ EN 1929 SOUS LE PSEUDONYME DE ELDER J.J. HADLEY: "QUAND IL DESCENDRA, SES CHEVEUX SERONT COMME LA LAINE DE L'AGNEAU, SES YEUX COMME LES FLAMMES DU FEU, ET TOUT HOMME SAURA QU'IL EST LE FILS DU VRAI DIEU VIVANT, IL Y AURA UN ARC-EN-CIEL AUTOUR DE LUI ET SES PIEDS SERONT COMME DU CUIVRE FIN... ET IL Y AURA UN ARBRE DEVANT LES DOUZE SORTES DE NOURRITURE, SES FEUILLES GUÉRIRONT DE LA DAMNATION, LE GRAND ROCHER OÙ S'ABRITER, LE VENT NE POURRA PLUS T'ATTEINDRE ET TU COMPTERAS LES QUATRE VINGT ANCIENS AVEC QUI TU POURRAS DISCUTER ET PARLER DES PROBLÈMES QUI T'AMÈNENT - LE MONDE D'OÙ TU VIENS."

R.Crumb

CHARLEY PATTON MOURUT LE 28 AVRIL 1934. SA MORT NE FUT RAPPORTÉE NULLE PART DANS LA PRESSE.

LA PLUPART DES INFORMATIONS CONTENUES DANS CETTE HISTOIRE PROVIENNENT DE L'EXCELLENT LIVRE DE ROBERT PALMER "DEEP BLUES" (VIKING PRESS, 1980)

226 Patton,
first appeared
in Zap 11,
1984.

PATTON
by R.Crumb

CHARLEY PATTON LIVED MOST OF HIS LIFE ON THE VAST DOCKERY PLANTATION IN THE BOTTOMLANDS OF THE MISSISSIPPI DELTA. HE WAS A RAMBLER, A SHIFTLESS NO-GOOD WHO LIVED OFF WOMEN AND PASSED HIS TIME IN TOTAL IDLENESS. HE WAS ALSO A GREAT BLUES PERFORMER WHOSE POWERFUL EFFECT ON THE BLUES AND ROCK AND ROLL IS STILL FELT TODAY, THOUGH FEW PEOPLE EVER HEARD OF HIM. THE MUSIC HE PLAYED AND SANG CAN IN NO WAY BE DESCRIBED, IT MUST BE LISTENED TO.

RECOMMENDED LISTENING: "CHARLEY PATTON" YAZOO L-1020, A DOUBLE ALBUM WITH 28 OF HIS RECORDED SONGS

227   Les As du Musette, Calendrier 2007,
Anthracite 2007.

229   Uncle Dave Macon, portrait, 2004.

230   R. Crumb's music sampler,
extra CD for Crumb Handbook, 2005.

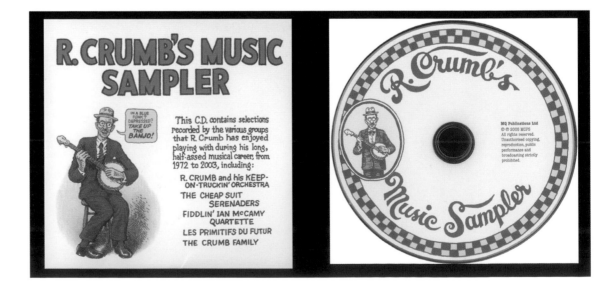

232   Janet Klein,
drawing, 2005.

228   Charlie Poole,
"You Ain't Talkin' To Me",
CD art, 2004.

231   Charlie Poole,
"You Ain't Talkin' To Me",
wooden CD box, Columbia, 2005.

233   Gus Viseur à Bruxelles,
CD cover, Paris Jazz Corner Productions, 1999.

234   Alan Lomax,
portrait, 2004.

235 Bad pop music is everywhere!, drawing, 2008.

236 Japanese Youths, drawing, 2007.

237 Portrait of Shelly, 2006.

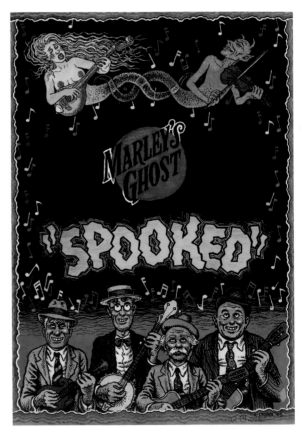

JELLY ROLL
MORTON

241 Potrait of an anony-
mous man with banjo, 2005.

ANONYMOUS MAN WITH BANJO
IN THIS PICTURE THE QUAINT CHARACTER IN HIS
RUSTIC SETTING FORMS A MOST INTRIGUING STUDY.

239 Jelly Roll
Morton, portrait,
2004.

240 Jelly Roll
Morton, portrait,
2004.

238 "Spooked", Marley's
Ghost, poster, 2005.

242 "Spooked", Marley's
Ghost, art work for CD cover,
Sage Arts Records, 2005.

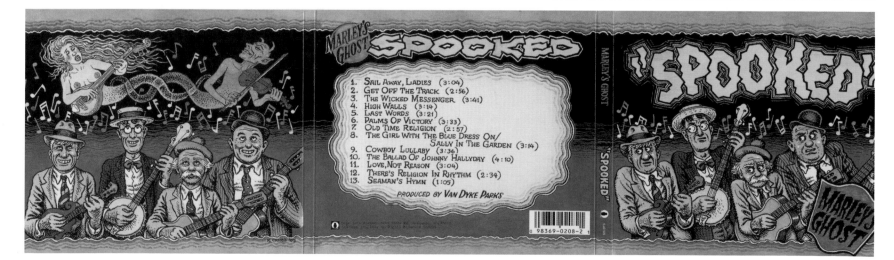

243   Paris, Plages d'Hawaii, CD cover,
Paris Jazz Corner Productions, 2005.

244   Eden & John's East River String
Band, Be Kind To a Man When He's
Down, CD and LP cover, ERR, 2011.

245   Tribal musette, CD cover,
Universal Music, 2008.

246 Eden & John's,
East River String Band,
concert poster (detail),
2008.

247 Eden & John's East River String Band,
"Some Cold Rainy Day", CD cover and LP, ERR, 2008.

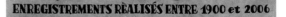

Méditerranée
ENREGISTREMENTS RÈALISÈS ENTRE 1939 et 2003

FRANCE: UNE ANTHOLOGIE DES MUSIQUES TRADITIONNELLES

Auvergne et Limousin
ENREGISTREMENTS RÈALISÈS ENTRE 1913 et 1998

FRANCE: UNE ANTHOLOGIE DES MUSIQUES TRADITIONNELLES

Bretagne
ENREGISTREMENTS RÈALISÈS ENTRE 1900 et 2006

FRANCE: UNE ANTHOLOGIE DES MUSIQUES TRADITIONNELLES

Corse
ENREGISTREMENTS RÈALISÈS ENTRE 1916 et 2009

FRANCE: UNE ANTHOLOGIE DES MUSIQUES TRADITIONNELLES

SINGER AT CAFÉ IN NIMES

HE LEANED OVER THE PEOPLE AT THE TABLES, HIS DELIVERY WAS EXTREMELY DRAMATIC, EMOTIONAL...

Centre France
ENREGISTREMENTS RÈALISÈS ENTRE 1909 et 1997

FRANCE: UNE ANTHOLOGIE DES MUSIQUES TRADITIONNELLES

249-258   Une Anthologie des
Musiques Traditionelles,
lettering for CD covers, 2009.

259   France, Une Anthologie
des Musiques Traditionelles,
art work for CD covers,
Fremeaux & Associes, 2009.

248   Singer at Café in Nimes,
placemat drawing, 2007.

France de l'ouest

ENREGISTREMENTS RÈALISÉS ENTRE 1956 et 2006

FRANCE: UNE ANTHOLOGIE DES MUSIQUES TRADITIONNELLES

France d'outre-mer

ENREGISTREMENTS RÈALISÉS ENTRE 1962 et 2007

FRANCE: UNE ANTHOLOGIE DES MUSIQUES TRADITIONNELLES

France

UNE ANTHOLOGIE DES MUSIQUES TRADITIONNELLES

Sud-ouest

ENREGISTREMENTS RÈALISÉS ENTRE 1939 et 2006

FRANCE: UNE ANTHOLOGIE DES MUSIQUES TRADITIONNELLES

Alpes, nord et est

ENREGISTREMENTS RÈALISÉS ENTRE 1930 et 2006

FRANCE: UNE ANTHOLOGIE DES MUSIQUES TRADITIONNELLES

Français d'Amérique

ENREGISTREMENTS RÈALISÉS ENTRE 1928 et 2004

FRANCE: UNE ANTHOLOGIE DES MUSIQUES TRADITIONNELLES

Welcome to the Saint

Notty's Jug Serenaders

ART by R. CRUMB '09

264   Peps Perssn, Heta Vax
Toast I Blue, record label,
Sweden, 1983.

265   Gérard Dôle,
Coeur de Patate Chaude,
CD cover, 2010.

266   Gérard Dôle,
Coeur de Patate Chaude,
CD label, 2010.

267   Festival M.A.D.
in Sauve, poster, 2009.

262   For record label Heta Vax, Sweden, 1983.

263   Eden & John's East River String Band,
"Drunken Barrel House Blues", CD cover, ERR, 2009.

260   Notty's Jug Serenaders,
Welcome to the Saint, CD cover,
Blue Monkey Records, 2009.

261   Eden & John's
East River String Band,
CD back cover, 2009.

THE GUY WITH THE BASS DRUM
WHO USED TO COME THROUGH THE NEIGHBORHOOD, SLOWLY
DOWN THE MIDDLE OF THE STREET... BOOM.....BOOM... YOU
COULD HEAR HIM COMING TWO OR THREE BLOCKS AWAY. US
LITTLE KIDS WERE TERRIFIED OF HIM AND WOULD RUN IN THE
HOUSE 'TIL HE PASSED BY. I ONLY ACTUALLY SAW HIM ONCE...
THE FIRST TIME WAS ENOUGH FOR ME. MY MOTHER SAID HE
WAS WALKING THROUGH THE NEIGHBORHOODS BEATING THAT BASS
DRUM WHEN SHE WAS A LITTLE GIRL.
— PHILADELPHIA, LATE '40S

BOOM

SHUMAN the HUMAN
WHAT A LIFE!
MR. UNCOOL HIMSELF! He's TOO... EXTREME!

267 Boom,
sketchbook, 2007.

R. Crumb,
The Complete Record Cover
Collection

Copyright © 2011, R. Crumb.
All rights reserved, first published by
Oog & Blik | De Bezige Bij,
Amsterdam, The Netherlands, 2011.
Introduction: Copyright © 2011,
Dominic Cravic.

All rights reserved

ISBN 978 0 393 08278 4

Published by arrangement with
Lora Fountain and Judy Hansen.

Book Design: Joost Swarte
with Nina Rödner
Production: Studio Peter de Raaf

www.oogenblik.nl

On the endpapers:
a composition of trading cards
from the box Les As du Musette,
Oog & Blik, Amsterdam, 1994.

W.W. Norton & Company, Inc.
500 Fifth Avenue, New York, N.Y.
10110
www.wwnorton.com

W.W. Norton & Company Ltd.
Castle House, 75/76 Wells Street,
London W1T 3QT

1 2 3 4 5 6